Hope...

Introduction

All perfect praise is due to Allaah, Who gives hope to the hopeful, The One Whose pleasure is sought by the devoted, ascetic worshippers. May Allaah exalt the mention of the noblest of all Prophets and Messengers, Muhammad, sallallaahu 'alayhi wa sallam, his Companions and all those who follow their footsteps, until the Day of Resurrection. We ask Allaah The Almighty to bestow His mercy upon us all, for He is indeed the Oft-forgiving and the Most Merciful.

To proceed:

In this book, we will address the subject of Rajaa' (hope), which is one of the deeds of the heart, and the most important of them all; having hope is an obligation, and one which must be directed to Allaah The Almighty alone.

Hope is necessary for those who are on the path of pleasing Allaah The Almighty, so that they may reach this goal (i.e. pleasing Allaah). If one loses hope in Allaah The Almighty for a second, then he will be ruined or almost ruined, because the state of a Muslim alternates between committing a sin which he hopes to be forgiven for, having a defect which he hopes to rectify, performing a good deed which he hopes shall be accepted, guidance which he hopes to achieve or closeness to Allaah The Almighty which he hopes to attain.

Therefore, hope is one of the most powerful means which help a

person on his path towards Allaah The Almighty; it also helps one maintain steadfastness on religion, especially during times like the ones we live in now, which are full of temptations, desires, trials and misconceptions. Hence a Muslim must try to possess all the means that would help him remain steadfast, and one of the most important of these is hope.

We must understand hope in a proper way in order to be among those who truly have hope, because if we misunderstand it then we would be among those who have wishful thoughts and false hopes.

Definition of hope

Linguistically: **Hope can mean wishing to achieve or obtain something, and it can also mean fearing something, as in the saying of Allaah The Almighty (which means):** {What is [the matter] with you that you do not fear the greatness of Allaah.} [QUR'AAN 71: 13] **The Arabic word 'Tarjoon' which is translated into fear comes from the original word 'Rajaa' which means 'hope', but also came to mean 'fear'.**

Terminologically: **Al-Manaawi, may Allaah have mercy upon him, said: "Hope refers to the attachment of the heart to something which one likes, and this attachment is evident and is reflected in one's conduct and behavior."** [1]

---

1 Faydh Al-Qadeer (67/5).

He, may Allaah have mercy upon him, also said: "It can also mean waiting for something which one likes and expects to occur, but one must have the means to achieve it. These means can be something like knowing the ability and power of Allaah and feeling the weakness of human beings and their continuous need for the help and support of Allaah." [1]

Ibn Al-Qayyim, may Allaah have mercy upon him, said: "Hope is when the heart longs for and is inclined towards something which one likes, and shunning anything that can prevent one from achieving that thing." [2]

He, may Allaah have mercy upon him, also said: "Hope is something that helps a person on towards what he likes, which is the pleasure of Allaah and admittance into Paradise, and it paves the way for him to achieve it and makes his journey pleasant. It was also said that hope is to wish for the generosity and kindness of Allaah. It was also said that hope is to place one's trust in Allaah." [3]

The opposite of having hope is to despair of the support and mercy of Allaah The Almighty, and to stop the heart from feeling the mercy Allaah. Despair is a sin, as Allaah The Almighty informs us in the story of Prophet Ya'qoob (Jacob),

---

1 Faydh Al-Qadeer (408/5).
2 Ar-Rooh (246).
3 Madaarij As-Saalikeen (35/2).

may Allaah exalt his mention, when Ya'qoob requested his children to search for Prophet Yoosuf (Joseph), may Allaah exalt his mention, and his brother. Allaah The Almighty Says (what means): {O my sons, go and find out about Yoosuf and his brother and despair not of relief from Allaah. Indeed, no one despairs of relief from Allaah except the disbelieving people.} [QUR'AAN 12: 87]

The difference between hope and wishful thinking

One must differentiate between hope and wishful thinking, because many people think that they have hope in Allaah and His mercy, while in reality they only have wishful thinking.

The difference between the two is that wishful thinking is accompanied with laziness with which one does not exert effort to achieve the sought objective. On the other hand, hope is when one wishes to achieve something and exerts the effort needed to achieve it.

Al-Manaawi, may Allaah have mercy upon him, said:
> "Having wishful thinking is dispraised, while having hope in Allaah is praiseworthy. This is because wishful thinking leads to laziness, which is contrary to hope, because hope makes the heart attached to Allaah and is reflected on one's conduct and behavior. Al-Ghazaali, may Allaah have mercy upon him, said: 'Hope, not

wishful thinking, is the starting point; for if a slave exerts effort in performing acts of obedience, then hopes that Allaah will accept his good deeds and forgive any shortcomings, this is true hope. On the other hand, if one is heedless and shuns obedience, commits different sins and does not care about the warnings of Allaah or the punishments awaiting the sinners and the negligent, and then after that he claims to hope that Allaah will admit him to Paradise and rescue him from the fire of Hell, this is nothing but wishful thinking which has no basis; and if one claims that it is hope, then he is misguided and upon great error." [1]

Allaah The Almighty clarified that the hope which believers have is that which is accompanied with action and deeds; He Says (what means): {Indeed, those who have believed and those who have emigrated and fought in the cause of Allaah, those hope for the mercy of Allaah. And Allaah is Forgiving and Merciful.} [QUR'AAN 2: 218] They first believed, then emigrated, then performed Jihaad in the path of Allaah; and Allaah The Almighty clarified that, having performed all these great actions and deeds, they hoped for His mercy.

Allaah The Almighty dispraised wishful thinking, Saying (what means): {It [i.e. Paradise] is not [obtained] by your wishful thinking nor by that of the People of the Scripture.

---

1 Faydh Al-Qadeer (67/5).

Al-Hasan, may Allaah have mercy upon him, said: "Faith is not [proved] by wishful thinking; rather it is something that is instilled in the heart and substantiated by actions and deeds." [1]

He, may Allaah have mercy upon him, also said: "[There were] some people who busied themselves with wishful thinking until they departed from this life having performed not one good deed. One of them said: 'I think good of my Lord [that Allaah The Almighty would forgive and pardon him].' He lied, because had he indeed had good thoughts, then he would have proven them by performing good deeds." [2]

Righteous people who possess pure hearts realize that this worldly life is the field in which to plant, in order to harvest the crops in the Hereafter; and they realize that the heart is like soil, and just like soil it must be planted with seeds in order to yield fruits, and it needs to be watered with acts of obedience for one to reap the rewards of the Hereafter. So that the soil may yield fruits, one must maintain it, protect it from harmful things and remove weeds and other plants which can weaken the tree and consume part of its fertilizer. This is also the case

---

1 Reported by Ibn Abi Abu Shaybah in his book Al-Musannaf (30351) and Al-Haakim in his book Shu'ab Al-Eemaan (66). Ibn Al-Qayyim classed it as authentic.
2 Reported by Al-Manaawi in his book Faydh Al-Qadeer (67/5).

with the believer; he purifies his heart from all doubts, misconceptions, desires and lusts so as to prevent these things from ruining the good deeds he planted and watered with the water of servitude. It is rare that one's belief would benefit him if his heart is corrupted, just like plants do not grow in a swampy land.

The slave's hope should be compared to that of a gardener; anyone who hopes to get good results in his plants should plant good seeds, water the plants whenever it is needed, maintain the plant, clear the land of thorns, weeds and anything which may harm it, and then wait and hope for the mercy and blessings of Allaah, Who will protect it from destructive thunderstorms and harmful pests until the plants grow strong and yield the fruits he hoped for: this is real hope in Allaah.

If one plants his seeds in a swampy land and sits waiting for it to grow and yield good fruits and crops, then he is a fool. If one plants in a good soil but never exerts any effort to make water reach it and claims to wait for the rains, then this is also wishful thinking and not hope.

When one utilizes all the available means and exerts all the efforts needed – which are within his capacity – leaving out nothing that a human being can exert and do, then, and only then, can he be said to have hope. This is the state of the believer: he exerts all efforts by performing acts of worship and obedience, and then expects the mercy of Allaah The Almighty, and that He will help him to remain steadfast, protect him from

erring and deviating from the path until his death, will not allow him to go astray and will take his soul while **He The Almighty is pleased with him.**

Allaah The Almighty dispraised people with wishful thinking from the previous nations, Saying (what means): *{And there followed them successors who inherited the Scripture [while] taking the commodities [i.e. unlawful gains and pleasures] of this lower life and saying: 'It will be forgiven for us.'}* [QUR'AAN 7: 169]

Allaah The Almighty also dispraised the owner of the garden, who said (what means): *{And I do not think the Hour will occur. And even if should be brought back to my Lord, I will surely find better than this as a return.}* [QUR'AAN 18: 36] **How could he expect to find anything good when he did not perform good deeds? This is merely false wishful thinking.**

We must beware of wishful thinking and exert all efforts and work hard, and perform our deeds in accordance with the Sunnah of the Prophet, sallallaahu 'alayhi wa sallam; and after this we can truly hope that Allaah The Almighty will grant us what is good in this life and the Hereafter.

Factors leading to achieving hope

Achieving hope in the heart of the believer requires factors that help him realize this. The scholars mentioned the four following

factors that help one achieve hope:

1. **Remembering the previous favors that Allaah The Almighty bestowed upon the slave:** The slave should remember and recollect the favors which Allaah The Almighty bestowed upon him in the past, including that He created him and provided him with hearing and sight; that He facilitated the earth for him to live in, revealed divine books and sent messengers to guide him to the right path and made him one of those who believe in Him and His great religion.

2. **Remembering the generosity of Allaah The Almighty and His promise of reward:** Allaah The Almighty has granted the slave things which he did not deserve and that he was not entitled to. Allaah The Almighty gives the slave more than what he deserves, despite his shortcomings regarding worship and obedience. If the slave remembers this generosity, he will have hope in more of this generosity and favors from Allaah The Almighty.

3. **Remembering the current favors of Allaah The Almighty:** Allaah The Almighty continues to bless us with different favors relating to both our religion and worldly life. His favors are endless in our bodies, senses, provisions, wealth, children and wives. Remembering the favors which one is enjoying now makes him hope for more favors and blessings in the future.

4. **Remembering the infinite mercy of Allaah The Almighty:** One should remember that the mercy of Allaah The Almighty precedes His wrath, and that He is The Most

Merciful and The Ever merciful, He is The Most Generous, The Companionate with His slave. Having hope in the heart depends on knowing the Names and Attributes of Allaah.

The sign of sound hope:

Ahmad ibn 'Aasim, may Allaah have mercy upon him, was asked: "What is the sign of having true hope?" He replied: "To be grateful when one is blessed with favors, to have hope that Allaah will perfect His favors upon him by granting more in this worldly life, and that He will forgive and pardon him in the Hereafter." [1]

The fruits of having hope:

Having hope has many great fruits and benefits, and the following are some of these fruits:

Starting to perform different acts of worship regularly:

Ibn Al-Qayyim, may Allaah have mercy upon him, said describing one of the types of people who return to the path of Allaah The Almighty: "Some of them return to Allaah by starting to perform acts of worship and deeds to come closer to Allaah. They are serious about worship and performing it is endeared to them. The source of this type of return to Allaah is having hope in Allaah, expecting His reward and the fulfillment

---

1 Mukhtasar Taareekh Dimashq (357).

of His promise." [1]

Enjoying acts of worship:

Ibn Al-Qayyim, may Allaah have mercy upon him, said: "Hope motivates the person who has hope while he is on the path to Allaah; it facilitates his journey and makes it enjoyable, encourages him, and helps him remain steadfast on the path and perform good deeds. If it was not for hope, then no one would have remained on the path of Allaah, because fear alone does not prompt the slave to perform (good) deeds. Rather, love prompts him, fear disturbs him and hope motivates him." [2]

Demonstrating servitude to Allaah:

Hope is one of the things that demonstrates the slave's servitude to Allaah The Almighty, shows his need of Allaah The Almighty, and confirms his inability to live without the favors, kindness and bounties of Allaah The Almighty even for the blink of an eye. Ibn Taymiyyah, may Allaah have mercy upon him, said: "The aspiration of the slave is that his Lord will forgive him, and his hope in Him entails his servitude to Him. On the other hand, if his heart turns away from seeking the forgiveness of Allaah and does not have hope in Him, then his heart will shift away from servitude to Allaah." [3]

---

1 Tareeq Al-Hijratayn (272).
2 Madaarij As-Saalikeen (50/2).
3 Al-Fataawa Al-Kubra (182/5).

Ibn Al-Qayyim, may Allaah have mercy upon him, said:
> "The slave submits to his Lord, surrenders his heart to Him and is content with what his Lord decrees for him, in hope that He will be merciful with him, pardon his shortcomings, forgive his sins, accept his good deeds (despite whatever defects they may have), and overlook his wrong deeds. The strong hope the slave has in his Lord entails this complete submission and surrender. It is not possible for any of this to happen if the slave has no hope in his Lord, because hope is the life of asking (from Allaah) and expecting that He responds (and fulfills the slave's needs), while having a strong will is its soul." [1]

Supplicating Allaah The Almighty:

Ibn Al-Qayyim, may Allaah have mercy upon him, said: "Supplication is based on having hope in Allaah. If the supplicating person does not hope that what he asking for will be given to him, then his heart will not be motivated to ask for it (in the first place). One does not usually ask for something if he does not expect it to be granted to him." [2]

Protecting oneself from the anger of Allaah The Almighty:

This point is based on the previous one. Allaah The Almighty loves for His slaves to supplicate Him, ask of Him, have hope in

---

1 Madaarij As-Saalikeen (45/2).
2 Badaa'i Al-Fawaa'id (523/3).

him and persist in their request and supplication. This is because He is The Most Generous, and The One Who gives abundantly to those who ask of Him. The most beloved thing to Allaah The Generous is that people ask of Him so that He gives them what they request and need. On the other hand, Allaah The Almighty becomes angry with those who do not ask of Him nor supplicate Him. Abu Hurayrah, may Allaah be pleased with him, narrated that the Messenger of Allaah, sallallaahu 'alayhi wa sallam, said: *"The person who does not ask from Allaah, Allaah becomes angry with him."* [1]

Learning the Attributes and Names of Allaah The Almighty:

The one who has hope in Allaah The Almighty is attached to His Names. For example, he is strongly attached to the Name 'The Most Generous' because he hopes in Allaah's generosity; he is attached in the Name 'The Most Merciful' because he hopes that He will forgive him; he is attached in the Name 'The Most Merciful' because he hopes to attain His mercy; he is attached in the Name 'The Oft-Forgiving' because he hopes that He will pardon him and accept his repentance. This encourages the slave to learn more about the Names of Allaah and His Attributes, and to understand them.

Obtaining what he asked of Allaah The Almighty:

If the slaves attaches his heart to his Lord, his Lord will grant him what he asks for. Ibn Al-Qayyim, may Allaah have mercy upon him, said: "The more the slaves thinks well of his Lord,

---

1 Reported by At-Tirmithi (3373) and Al-Albaani classed it as authentic.

has hope in Him (to fulfill his needs) and sincerely relies on Him, [the more] Allaah will not turn him down nor disappoint him, because Allaah does not allow anyone's deeds and effort to go to waste or be lost." [1]

When the slave gets what he asked for and his request is answered by Allaah The Almighty, he becomes more attached to Him, supplicates Him more, has more hope in Him, relies more on Him, and is encouraged to perform more good deeds. The best thing that a slave can hope for from his Lord is that his Lord may be pleased with him, admit him into Paradise and bless him with the favor of seeing Him in Paradise. Therefore, one should have hope that his Lord will grant him such blessings, so that they may be bestowed upon him.

Loving Allaah The Almighty:

This is a natural result of the previous point, because when Allaah The Almighty grants the slave what he asks for, the slave becomes more attached to Allaah The Almighty, loves Him and is content with Him.

Thanking Allaah The Almighty:

Obtaining what one asks from Allaah The Almighty makes the slave grateful, and gratitude is one of the highest levels of servitude.

---

1 Madaarij As-Saalikeen (471/1).

Mentioning Allaah The Almighty frequently:

Having hope in Allaah The Almighty entails that one always expect to receive what he asked for and anticipate the favors of Allaah The Almighty. This entails that the slave becomes more attached to his Lord and turns to Him frequently. One has many things to ask from Allaah The Almighty; one hopes that Allaah The Almighty will make him successful in his studies, grant him a job after that, bless him with a good wife, give him children and guide him to the right path. Thus, one spends one's entire life attached to Allaah The Almighty, having hope in Him.

Fluctuating between hope and fear

Al-'Ayni, may Allaah have mercy upon him, said:
> "If one realizes how boundless the mercy of Allaah is, he will never lose hope; if he realizes how severe the punishment of Allaah is, he will always be fearful of Him. Therefore, [the state of] the slave should always fluctuate between fear and hope. One should not exaggerate in having hope to the point that he becomes like the Murji'ah (a deviant sect), who claim that if one believes then it does not matter what he does after that; neither should one exaggerate in fearing Allaah, to the point that he becomes like the Khawaarij and the Mu'tazilah (two other deviant sects), who claim that one will stay in Hell eternally if one commits any of the grave

> major sins and dies without repenting. One should choose the middle ground, as Allaah The Almighty Says (what means): {They hope for His mercy and fear His punishment.} [QUR'AAN 17: 57]."[1]

This is a very important rule which every believing slave must establish in his heart. The state of the slave always fluctuates between hope and fear; in his heart, he combines hope in Allaah The Almighty and His Mercy and fear of Allaah The Almighty and His punishment. When the slave achieves this balance, then his faith is sound.

Abu 'Ali Ar-Rawthabaari, may Allaah have mercy upon him, said: "Hope and fear are like the two wings of a bird, if they are balanced, then the bird flies perfectly, and if either of the two has a defect, then it will not be able to fly; and if the bird loses both, then it will die. This is why it was said before, that if the believer's fear and hope were to be measured and weighed, then they would be equal." [2]

Combining fear and hope is the method of the verses of the Qur'aan. An-Nawawi, may Allaah have mercy upon him, said: "Most of the verses of the Qur'aan combine between fear and hope." [3]

---

[1] 'Umdat al Qaari (23/66-67).
2 Reported by Al-Bayhaqi in his book Shu'ab Al-Eemaan (1027).
3 The explanation of An-Nawawi on the book of Muslim (73/17).

Allaah The Almighty Says (what means): {*On the Day [some] faces will turn white and [some] faces will turn black.*} [QUR'AAN 3: 106] **Allaah The Almighty gives His slaves hope in having white (bright) faces, and frightens them from the prospect of having black (gloomy) faces on the Day of Resurrection.**

Allaah The Almighty also Says (what means): {*Indeed, your Lord is swift in penalty; but indeed, He is Forgiving and Merciful.*} [QUR'AAN 7: 167] **Allaah The Almighty combines between giving people hope in His mercy, and frightening them with a swift penalty.**

Allaah The Almighty Says (what means): {*Indeed, the righteous will be in pleasure. And indeed, the wicked will be in Hellfire.*} [QUR'AAN 82: 13-14]

He also Says (what means): {*Then as for one whose scales are heavy [with good deeds], He will be in a pleasant life. But as for one, whose scales are light, His abode will be an abyss [i.e. the pit of Hellfire].*} [QUR'AAN 101: 6-9]

There are a great many verses on this issue, which combine between fear and hope. This can occur within the same verse or in consecutive verses.

Fear results in hope and hope results in fear; because every

person who has fear has hope (that Allaah The Almighty will save him), or else he will despair. The best time to have hope is when one is afraid. Ibn Taymiyyah, may Allaah have mercy upon him, said: "Fear always includes hope or else one would despair. Likewise, hope entails fear, or else one would feel secure from the punishment of Allaah (and thus refrain from performing good deeds and avoiding sins). Those who fear Allaah and have hope in Him are the knowledgeable people whom Allaah praised (in the Qur'aan)." [1]

Some people deviated in this regard in two extremes. Al-'Ayni, may Allaah have mercy upon him, detailed the beliefs held by two groups, saying:

> "One group made hope overwhelm fear, and the second group made fear overwhelm hope. The truth which Ahlus-Sunnah (The People of Prophetic Tradition) is upon is that one should combine between the two and balance them. One may read in the books of some of the scholars where they state that fear should be dominant, and read of others who state that hope should be dominant. However, this is not the same deviation which some sects fell in. Ibn Al-Qayyim said: 'Righteous people were divided into two groups in the race towards Allaah: some were worried and thus were saying (with fear) that if Allaah does not forgive them, then they will certainly go to Hell. Other made hope dominant, like Bilaal, may Allaah be pleased with him, whose wife was sad at the

---

1 Majmoo' Al-Fataawa (21/7).

time of his death and said this aloud in front of him, but he was happy and had great hopes, and said: 'Tomorrow (after his death) I will meet my beloved ones, Muhammad and his Companions (i.e. in Paradise).'" [1]

The third opinion is the one which states that a person should not allow either of the two feelings to be dominant over the other but should maintain a balance at all times, except in certain conditions (which will be mentioned later on).

Means that can help one balance hope and fear

There are different things that Allaah The Almighty made means which help people to maintain such a balance.

One of these is that Allaah The Almighty does not give people knowledge of how they will end their lives, which will keep them fluctuating always between fear and hope. Ibn Battaal, may Allaah have mercy upon him, said: "There is a great wisdom behind not informing people upon which deed they will end their lives; it reflects gentleness and wisdom because, were people to know this, then the ones who are to be saved (from Hell) among them will become lazy and never exert an effort, and those who are destined to go to Hell will become even more evil (as nothing will help them). Therefore, concealing this from

____

1 Badaa'i Al-Fawaa'id (735/3).

people keeps them between the states of fear and hope all the time." [1]

Some scholars explained this in a different way, saying: "An eclipse is an indication that the slave must be in a state of fear and hope all the time. Ibn Hajar, may Allaah have mercy upon him, said: 'One of the wisdoms behind an eclipse is to indicate to people that they must always be between the states of fear and hope, because an eclipse happens (which puts the slave in fear) and then it is gone (which gives hope again).'" [2]

When an eclipse takes place the believer goes into a state of fear of his Lord, because an eclipse reflects the might and greatness of Allaah, and that He is capable of destroying these signs that show His greatness and ability to create; He is capable of destroying the entire earth and all who live on it; He is capable of destroying the heavens and cause them to collapse on the earth. It is these aspects that put the believer in a state of fear; however, he keeps hope in Allaah The Almighty to remove this eclipse and bring back light to this planet so that people could benefit from it. This is how the slave may combines between the state of fear and hope in the event of such an eclipse.

Al-Manaawi, may Allaah have mercy upon him, said: "The path leading to security (in the Hereafter) is a path between two

---

1 Fat-h Al-Baari (330/11).
2 Fat-h Al-Baari (532/2).

terrifying paths: the path of feeling secure (of being punished) and the path of despair (of the mercy of Allaah). The path that combines between fear and hope is the middle path that leads to security (in the Hereafter). When one loses hope altogether, he lands on the path of fear (i.e. despair) and when one loses fear altogether, he lands on the path of feeling secure (from punishment). The upright path is the one between these two extremes, and if one deviates to the right or to the left of it, he will be destroyed. Therefore, one should have both feelings present at the same time (i.e. fear and hope) and take this fine path (towards true security)." [1]

The scholars mentioned that there are situations where one should make hope dominate fear, and others when he should make fear dominate hope. This could be seen as a treatment that is used to cure a particular ailment.

> Al-Maawurdi, may Allaah have mercy upon him, said: "Fear and hope are two medicines, but for two people with opposite diseases. If the doctor is ignorant or false, he will use the wrong medicine for the wrong disease." [2]

However, this does not mean that one should make one of the two feelings dominate the other all the time, as some of the

---

1 Faydh Al-Qadeer (78/2).
2 Faydh Al-Qadeer (369/6).

people of Bid'ah (innovation in religion) did, thus deviating from the right path. Rather, it should be done according to the situation and the need of the slave.

Examples of situations when the slave should make hope dominate fear:

- **At the time of death:**

Abu Hurayrah, may Allaah be pleased with him, narrated that the Prophet of Allaah, sallallaahu 'alayhi wa sallam, said that Allaah The Almighty Says: *"I will be [for My slave] as My slave thinks of Me."* [1]

Waathilah ibn Al-Asqa', may Allaah be pleased with him, narrated: "I heard the Messenger of Allaah, sallallaahu 'alayhi wa sallam, say that Allaah The Almighty Says: *"I am just as My slave thinks I am [i.e. I will do for him what he thinks I can do for him] so let him think of whatever he wishes."* [2]

In these two narrations, hope dominates fear, as Al-Karmaani, may Allaah have mercy upon him, said: "These narrations

---

1 Reported by Al-Bukhaari (7505) and Muslim (2675).
2 Reported by Ahmad (16059) and Al-Haakim classed it as authentic and Ath-Thahabi approved his ruling.

indicate that one should make hope dominate fear." [1]

The scholars said that this happens at the time of one's death, and used the following narration as evidence to prove their statement; Jaabir ibn 'Abdullaah, may Allaah be pleased with him, narrated: "I heard the Messenger of Allaah, sallallaahu 'alayhi wa sallam, say three nights before his death: *'None of you should die except that he thinks the best of Allaah.'* [2]

An-Nawawi, may Allaah have mercy upon him, said: "It is recommended that people remind the person at the time of his death to think good of Allaah The Almighty. It is also recommended to mention the good deeds he (the dying person) used to perform in order to help him think good of Allaah The Almighty and die on this state. This is a recommended thing to do according to the consensus of the scholars." [3]

Thinking well of Allaah The Almighty is essential at all times. However, making hope dominate fear should only be done at the time of death, when one is approaching his Lord. This is why some of the Salaf (righteous predecessors) used to command their children to recite the verses of mercy at the time of their death, so that their souls would depart while they have good thoughts of Allaah The Almighty and the firm belief that He would forgive them, have mercy upon them and accept

---

1 'Umdat Al-Qaari (101/25).
2 Reported by Muslim (2877).
3 The explanation of An-Nawawi on the book of Muslim (138/2).

them. [1]

Ash-Shaafi'i, may Allaah have mercy upon him, was asked during his death illness: "O Abu 'Abdullaah, how is your situation this morning?" He replied: "I woke up in the process of departing from this worldly life, will be separated from my brothers, will taste the bitterness of death, will face the consequence of my misdeeds and will be brought to stand in front of Allaah. I do not know whether my soul is going to be taken to Paradise so I may congratulate it, or to Hell so that may I condole it." Then he, may Allaah have mercy upon him, started to weep.

One may ask: why should one make hope dominate fear in such situations?

An-Nawawi, may Allaah have mercy upon him, answered this question, saying: "When the signs of death becomes evident, one should make hope dominate fear, or rather stop fear completely and feel nothing but hope. This is because the objective of feeling fear is to refrain from sins and wrongdoing, and perform more good deeds, and this does not exist at the time of death. Therefore, it becomes recommended for one to think the best of his Lord. Thinking well of our Lord makes one feel his great need of Allaah The Almighty and makes one submit to Him." [2]

---

1 Shu'ab Al-Eemaan (1008) and Hilyat Al-Awliyaa' (31/3).
2 The explanation of An-Nawawi on the book of Muslim (210/17).

- When people despair of the mercy of Allaah The Almighty due to their sins:

Some people may despair of the mercy of Allaah The Almighty because of sins and misdeeds that they have committed; in this case, hope should be made to dominate fear. Such people should be reminded of the forgiveness of Allaah The Almighty and His pardon, and that repentance eradicates previous sins.

Al-Manaawi, may Allaah have mercy upon him, said: "Fear and hope are parallel; however, at the time of fear and feeling despair, then hope should be made dominant." [1]

Examples of situations when the slave should make fear dominate hope:

- When people lead a relaxed and luxurious life:

An-Nawawi, may Allaah have mercy upon him, said: "The scholars said: 'It is recommended for the one who is admonishing people to combine fear and hope in his speech, to avoid making people either despair of the mercy of Allaah or feel secure from His punishment. However, fear should be more in his speech than hope, because the souls are in more need of hearing things that would frighten them than things that would make them feel safe from punishment. This is because people

---

1 Faydh Al-Qadeer (446/2).

are (by nature) relaxed, negligent, have strong hope and neglect performing good deeds.'" [1]

* When one commits sins:

If one commits a sin, then he should remember the wrath and punishment of Allaah The Almighty; he should remember the fire of Hell and its torment; he should hasten to repentance, return to the path of Allaah The Almighty and shun all evil.

It is amazing how some people nowadays commit sins and yet harbor hopes of Allaah's mercy and forgiveness; this is foolishness and pure ignorance of the might of Allaah The Almighty.

Ibn Al-Qayyim, may Allaah have mercy upon him, said:
> "Some people hold on to the texts (Qur'aanic verses and Prophetic narrations) of hope (in the mercy of Allaah) and rely on them and hang on to them with both hands. If someone reproaches them because of the sins that they commit, they start listing the texts that they have memorized, which address the issue from the angle of hope and the infinite mercy of Allaah. Some of these ignorant people say: 'Refraining from sins is actually a form of ignorance of the vast forgiveness of Allaah.' Another one says: 'Shunning sins is a way of undermining the forgiveness of Allaah.'

---

1 The explanation of An-Nawawi on the book of Muslim (73/17).

"Muhammad ibn Hazm, may Allaah have mercy upon him, said: 'I heard one of these ignorant people say in his supplications: 'O Allaah, I seek refuge in You from not committing sins.'

"These people deceive themselves and live in delusions and false hopes. It is amazing what delusion and deception can do to a person. Thinking well of Allaah benefits the person who actually repents to Allaah, regrets what he did, refrains from sinning, replaces misdeeds with good deeds and continues the remaining part of their life in obedience and virtue. After all of this, one can think good of his Lord; otherwise it is nothing but (self) deception.

"There is a great difference between thinking well of Allaah and being deceived. The knowledgeable person places hope in its appropriate place, while the ignorant one puts it in the wrong place." [1]

- **When people feel secure of being punished by Allaah The Almighty:**

A committed and devout Muslim who is upon obedience and continuously works to attain the love of Allaah The Almighty may slip into feeling this way. He may feel secure of being

---

1 Al-Jawaab Al-Kaafi (15/11).

punished, because of the good deeds he has accumulated and because he can see that he is always performing righteous deeds. Whenever the heart starts to incline towards this feeling, one should hasten in making the feeling of fear dominate hope and must remember the punishment of Allaah The Almighty, and how He could progressively lead them to destruction by trying and testing them with one favor after another. One should remember that there are people who perform good deeds, but then end their lives in an evil and bad manner. Thinking of these possibilities would enable a person to cleanse his heart from the rust that covers it and make fear dominate hope, until these deceptive feelings of security from Allaah's punishment go away.

Al-Manaawi, may Allaah have mercy upon him, said: "Fear and hope are parallel; however, at the time of fear hope should be dominant, and at the time of hope and feeling secure fear should be made dominant." [1]

The different types of hope

In light of what we have said so far, one can say that there are three types of hope: two praised types, and one dispraised.

The two praised types:

1. The hope of a person who is upon obedience, performs

---

1 Faydh Al-Qadeer (446/2).

good deeds and performs them correctly (i.e. according to what Allaah The Almighty legislated); such a person can hope for the reward of Allaah The Almighty.

2. The hope of a person who committed sins and then repented; such a person can hope for the forgiveness of Allaah The Almighty and that Allaah The Almighty will conceal his sins and eradicate them.

The dispraised type:

1. The hope of a person who continuously sins and commits misdeeds, and then hopes in the mercy and forgiveness of Allaah The Almighty without performing any good deed; these are false hopes and a deception.

Abu 'Uthmaan Al-Hayri, may Allaah have mercy upon him, said the following profound words in this regard: "A sign of being blessed is when one performs good deeds but fears that he will not be accepted. A sign of misery is when one performs misdeeds and hopes that he will be saved (from the punishment of Allaah)." [1]

A question that arises here is, which one of the two praised types of hope is greater in reward?

The scholars differed which of the two is greater and more rewarding: is it the one of the person who performs good deeds

---

1 Fat-h Al-Baari (301/11).

and hopes to be rewarded, or the one of the person who sins but then repents and hopes to be forgiven?

A group of the scholars ruled the first type to be better, because the reasons for the person being hopeful are strong as he performs righteous deeds and his hope is realistic. On the other hand, another group of scholars ruled the second type to be better, because such a person feels a great need for Allaah The Almighty and experiences shame and mortification whenever he remembers his sins; this type of hope has no room for arrogance or (self) deception, because such a person did not yet perform good deeds by which he could be deceived.

Both opinions may be true, but a Muslim should maintain a balance and combine between the two types of hope. Whenever Allaah The Almighty blesses him and enables him to perform good deeds, then he can hope for the reward of these deeds and he can hope to be admitted into Paradise. However, if he slips and commits a sin, then he should repent and have hope that Allaah The Almighty will forgive his sins.

The different levels of hope

Hope has three different levels and they differ in the outcome:

First: The hope of a person who exerts hard efforts in worship:
This generates certain sweetness to the worship despite the difficulty and hardship accompanying the deed. He who knows the reward and outcome of the effort he is exerting will exert

even more. The one who hopes to attain high profits as a result of a trip, will endure the hardships he faces during his journey. This is just like a businessman who travels, stays up at night and puts up with many difficulties because of the profit he is expecting as a result of the journey.

Likewise is the case of a person who loves Allaah The Almighty and strives to attain His pleasure; this person will find no difficulty waking up for the Fajr prayer, performing Wudhoo' during cold seasons, performing Jihaad, performing Hajj or 'Umrah, seeking knowledge despite the hardships, performing voluntary night prayers, feeling hunger when fasting and so on. As a matter of fact, the hardship and difficulties that accompany performing these good deeds eventually turn into joy and pleasure.

The normal steps when performing deeds is that one faces difficulties and feels burdened in the beginning, but then one starts enjoying what he does. One of the scholars said: "I endured the hardship of waking up for the night prayers for twenty continuous years, but then I enjoyed praying for the twenty years after that." [1] The slave will not be able to taste the sweetness of worship unless he suffers and endures its hardship first.

When one has a strong hope in the reward resulting from the deed, then he will be able to abandon rest and what he used to.

---

1 Lataa'if Al-Ma'aarif (43).

When one realizes the magnitude of the reward, it becomes easy for them to give up their wealth and spend it for the sake of Allaah The Almighty.

When one is aware of the greatness of the reward, it becomes easy for them to fast and give up food, drinks and having intercourse with their spouse.

When one is mindful of the reward of perseverance and being content with what Allaah The Almighty decrees for him, they are able to endure the pain of hardship, to the point that bitter feelings become as sweet as honey.

It is in man's nature that he cannot give up something that he likes unless he gets something greater in return; in this case, this greater thing, so dear to the hearts, is attaining the pleasure of Allaah The Almighty, His Paradise and an abundant reward.

Second: The hope of a person who gives up things that he likes:
Those who strive and struggle against themselves in order to give up something they like, and replace it with something better and greater in reward. Their hope is to achieve this goal, but they need (Islaamic) knowledge in order to know which is better and more rewarding before they are able to replace something with another.

Third: The hope to meet Allaah The Almighty:

Those who are eager to meet Allaah and long for His meeting will give up this worldly life completely; this is the highest of the three levels of hope. Allaah The Almighty Says (what means): {So whoever would hope for the meeting with his Lord, let him do righteous work and not associate in the worship of his Lord anyone.} [QUR'AAN 18:110] Allaah The Almighty also Says (what means): {Whoever should hope for the meeting with Allaah - indeed, the term [decreed by] Allaah is coming And He is the Hearing, the Knowing.} [QUR'AAN 29:5]

Hoping to meet Allaah The Almighty (and attain His pleasure and Paradise) is the essence of faith; it is for this that devout worshippers strive and exert great efforts and it is meeting that makes difficult things easy and enjoyable. This is why Allaah The Almighty set a time when this will happen, so that they can work to achieve this goal and attain this great prize.

Those in this level of hope remain eager and restless until the meeting happens, because they always long for the meeting. They continuously prepare themselves for this meeting and their hearts always wonder, when would this meeting take place? When will they meet Allaah The Almighty? Meeting Allaah for these people is greater than all the pleasure in Paradise.

The story of one of the Companions illustrates this level of

hope. 'Umayr ibn Al-Humaam Al-Ansaari, may Allaah be pleased with him, so longed to meet Allaah The Almighty that he felt that eating a few dates would delay him from this meeting.

Anas, may Allaah be pleased with him, reported that the Messenger of Allaah, sallallaahu 'alayhi wa sallam, and his Companions reached (the area of) Badr before the polytheists, and when they arrived, he, sallallaahu 'alayhi wa sallam, directed: *"Let no one of you advance ahead of me."* When the polytheists came near, the Messenger of Allaah, sallallaahu 'alayhi wa sallam, said: *"Now stand up and proceed towards Jannah [Paradise] which is as wide as are the heavens and the earth."* `Umayr ibn Al-Humaam, may Allaah be pleased with him, asked: "Is Jannah as wide as are the heaven and the earth?" The Messenger of Allaah, sallallaahu 'alayhi wa sallam, replied in the affirmative. `Umayr remarked: "Great!" The Messenger of Allaah, sallallaahu 'alayhi wa sallam, asked him what had urged him to say so. He replied: "Nothing, O Messenger of Allaah! But hope that I might become one of the inhabitants of Jannah." The Messenger of Allaah, sallallaahu 'alayhi wa sallam, said: *"You will definitely be among them."* `Umayr then took some dates out of his quiver and began to eat them, but after a short time he said: "If I survive until I eat my dates, it will mean a long life." So he threw away the dates which he had with him and then fought with the enemy till he was killed. [1]

---

1 Reported by Muslim (1901).

Allaah The Almighty Knew that this category of believers long to meet Him (and they are rare), and that their souls are eager for this meeting, He The Almighty set a time for them in order that their souls relax and exert efforts with hope; Allaah Said (what means): {Whoever should hope for the meeting with Allaah - indeed, the term [decreed by] Allaah is coming And He is the Hearing, the Knowing.} [Qur'aan 29:5]

There is a drastic difference between people today and the righteous Salaf in this regard. People nowadays are heedless of this matter and they never give it the slightest thought; whereas it was always in the hearts and minds of the Companions and was encouraged in the Qur'aan and the Sunnah. We ask Allaah The Almighty to makes us among them and make us of those whose ambition help him elevate in the ranks and the levels of hope and worship.

Hope and sins

A sin, regardless of how great and grave it is, can still be forgiven and the door of hope is wide open for those who repent. People should not despair and think that they are absolutely destroyed and ruined; rather they should rush and repent from their sins and put their hope in the mercy of Allaah. Allaah made the door of forgiveness open for all kinds of sins; Allaah The Almighty Says (what means): {Say, 'O My servants who have transgressed against themselves [by

sinning] do not despair of the mercy of Allaah. Indeed, Allaah forgives all sins [for those who repent]. Indeed, it is He who is the Forgiving, the Merciful.'} [QUR'AAN 39:53] **This is not addressing those who committed a minor sin, but rather those who transgressed against themselves by committing many sins. The door for forgiveness is open for those who repent and return to Allaah.**

Allaah The Almighty also Says (what means): {And when those come to you [O Muhammad] who believe in Our verses, say: 'Peace be upon you. Your Lord has decreed upon Himself mercy: that any of you who does wrong out of ignorance and then repents after that and corrects himself, indeed, He is Forgiving and Merciful.'} [QUR'AAN 6:54] **Ibn Jareer, may Allaah have mercy upon him, commented on this verse saying: "O Muhammad, when those who believe in what We revealed and in Our signs and admit to this belief and practice it, if they come to you asking guidance regarding their sins and what they did before and whether or not their repentance would accepted, then do not cause them to despair. Tell them O Muhammad, peace and security is upon you from Allaah regarding your sins; He will not punish you for them after repenting from them because He has decreed upon Himself mercy when dealing with His slaves."** [1]

Allaah The Almighty also Says (what means): {And [there are]

---

1 Tafseer At-Tabari (205/5).

others who have acknowledged their sins. They had mixed [i.e. polluted] a righteous deed with another that was bad. Perhaps Allaah will turn to them in forgiveness. Indeed. Allaah is Forgiving and Merciful. Take [O Muhammad], from their wealth a charity by which you purify them and cause them increase. and invoke [Allaah's blessings] upon them. Indeed. your invocations are reassurance for them. And Allaah is Hearing and Knowing.] [QUR'AAN 9:102-103] **Ibn Jareer, may Allaah have mercy upon him, commented on this verse saying: "Allaah is referring to mixing the sin of abstaining from the battle of Tabook and not participating in Jihaad with the Muslims, with their acknowledgement of these sins and repentance from them. Then He informed them that He will forgive them because they acknowledged of these sins and repented from them."** [1]

Anas, may Allaah be pleased with him, said: "I heard the Messenger of Allaah, sallallaahu 'alayhi wa sallam, saying: 'Allaah. the Exalted. has said: `O son of Aadam! I shall go on forgiving you so long as you pray to Me and aspire for My forgiveness. whatever your sins may be. O son of Adam! I do not care even if your sins should pile up to the sky and should you beg pardon of Me. I would forgive you. O son of Adam! If you come to Me with an earth-full of sins and meet Me. not

---

1 Tafseer At-Tabari (459/6).

associating anything with Me in worship, I will certainly grant you as much pardon as will fill the earth.'" [1] **In this narration, Allaah The Almighty opens the gate of hope for His slaves.**

Ibn `Umar, may Allaah be pleased with him, reported: "I heard Messenger of Allaah, sallallaahu 'alayhi wa sallam, saying: 'A believer will be brought close to his Lord on the Day of Resurrection and enveloping him in His Mercy. He will make him confess his sins by saying: 'Do you remember (doing) this sin and this sin?' He will reply: 'My Lord, I remember.' Then He will say: 'I covered it up for you in the life of world, and I forgive it for you today.' Then the record of his good deeds will be handed to him. As for the disbelievers and the hypocrites; the witnesses will say: 'These are the ones who lied against their Lord. Unquestionably, the curse of Allaah is upon the wrongdoers.'"

One can attain all this mercy and forgiveness if one truly repents; if one submits oneself to Allaah The Almighty; if one supplicates Allaah The Almighty; if one exerts efforts in performing acts of obedience; if one refrains from sinning; if one regrets what one did and starts a new life; and if one is determined never to go back to what one used to do.

---

1 Reported by At-Tirmithi (3540) and Al-Albaani classed it as authentic.
4 Reported by Al-Bukhaari (2768) and Muslim (2441).

One must strive hard and not waste the chance that one has; and one must know that when death comes, they will regret wasting this chance and wish that they could be brought back so they could utilize it; but it would be too late then, as the time for work and struggle would have run out, and the time for questioning would have begun.

Hope as a treatment

Hope is a cure which two types of people need:

- A person who has despaired to the point that he has given up worship altogether, convinced that it is of no use or benefit.

- A person whose fear of punishment has dominated him to the point that he harms himself and those under his guardianship. His fear may have exceeded the permissible limit; therefore, he must be reminded to have hope and to maintain a balance between fear and hope.

As for the deceived sinner who has false hopes while shunning worship of and obedience to Allaah The Almighty, attempting to motivate such a person with hope will be of no avail and could even worsen his state. One should only use fear to admonish such people; they should be rebuked, warned and reminded of the time of death.

A person who admonishes people should maintain a balance when addressing them, not to scare them too much and lead them to despair, and not to give them very high hopes and lead them to become negligent.

Some scholars said: "A person who admonishes others should be kind to them and treat every problem (of theirs) suitably."

'Ali ibn Abi Taalib, may Allaah be pleased with him, said: "The one with real knowledge is he who admonishes people and does not make them despair of the mercy of Allaah, does not give them permission to commit sins, does not make them feel secure of the punishment of Allaah and does not shun the Qur'aan and resort to something else in its place (i.e. feeling that there is something else which can admonish people that is better than the Qur'aan)." [1]

> Sufyaan ibn 'Uyaynah, may Allaah have mercy upon him, said: "He who admonishes people and makes them (and himself) despair of the mercy of Allaah commits a serious error." [2]

Zayd ibn Aslam, may Allaah have mercy upon him, said: "There was a man from the previous nations who was a diligent worshipper. He would exhaust himself in worship and would

---

1 Reported by Ad-Daarami (304).
2 Tafseer Ibn Abu Haatim (65/9).

address people and make them despair of the mercy of Allaah. This man died and (on the Day of Resurrection) he said: 'O my Lord, what is my abode?' Allaah said: 'Hell fire.' The man asked: 'What happened to my worship and the effort I used to exert?' He was told: 'You used to make people despair of My Mercy, and today you will despair of My Mercy.'" [1]

Therefore, one must maintain a balance according to the situation of the people he is addressing. If they are negligent people and commit sins, then he may scare them, but if they are people who fear Allaah The Almighty, then he should give them hope.

Matters related to hope

- Hope is connected to present and previous deeds:

When a believer performs a deed, he hopes that Allaah The Almighty will accept it and reward him for it. Some people limit their hope to the time of the event and after they perform a deed they forget it. This is not how the believer should be; the believer should have hope in Allaah The Almighty, that He will accept and reward them for their previous good deeds, and they should also fear being punished for their previous sins.

Ibn Taymiyyah, may Allaah have mercy upon him, said: "Fear

---

1 Tafseer 'Abdur-Razzaaq (236/3).

and hope are connected to both the present and the previous deeds, because the consequence of these deeds is in the future. One hopes that Allaah has accepted his previous good deeds and will reward him for it in the future, and fears that Allaah did not accept his deeds and will be deprived from its reward (in the future)." [1]

- ## Hope regarding worldly matters:

Hope is not limited to the matters that are related to the Hereafter; rather, it applies to worldly matters as well. A person may hope that Allaah The Almighty would bless him with wealth, children, a spouse, a job, a cure from an illness, or finding something that he may have lost. Prophet Ya'qoob, may Allaah exalt his mention, applied hope to worldly matters; Allaah The Almighty Says (what means): {'O my sons, go and find out about Yoosuf and his brother and despair not of relief from Allaah. Indeed, no one despairs of relief from Allaah except the disbelieving people.'} [QUR'AAN 12:87] Prophet Ya'qoob, may Allaah exalt his mention, instructed his children not to despair from finding Yoosuf, may Allaah exalt his mention, and his brother, and this is a worldly matter.

Ibn Jareer, may Allaah have mercy upon him, said: "Prophet Ya'qoob, may Allaah exalt his mention, was hopeful of finding his son (Prophet) Yoosuf, and so he told his children to go back

---

1 Majmoo' Al-Fataawa (452/7).

to where they came from, to the place where they had left their brothers behind. He instructed them not to despair in the mercy of Allaah nor lose hope; perhaps Allaah would relief his sadness due to losing Yoosuf and his brother; {And despair not of relief from Allaah.} He was hopeful that Allaah would bring them back and he would see them again, and he never lost hope because; {No one despairs of relief from Allaah except the disbelieving people.} [1]

Having hope in Allaah The Almighty regarding worldly matters is very important, because when the believer's hope in Allaah The Almighty decreases regarding worldly matters, then he starts to have what is known as hidden doubt (in Allaah The Almighty and His ability). A person whose hope in Allaah The Almighty is perfect will have his heart attached and dependent on Him alone, not to mere human beings. However, if his hope in Allaah The Almighty decreases, then his heart will become attached and dependent on human beings, in the hope that they would fulfill his worldly needs. This is the hidden doubt which most people fall into, except those whom Allaah The Almighty protects and guards. [2]

- ### Hope continues after death:

When the slave dies and reaches his Lord, his hope increases if

---

1 Tafseer At-Tabari (284/7).
2 Majmoo' Al-Fataawa (94/1).

he was a righteous person (in his worldly life). When the time comes for a hired person to receive his wages, his hope that he will get what he worked for becomes stronger; likewise, when the righteous people stand before their Lord, they become even more hopeful of receiving their reward.

The Prophet of Allaah, sallallaahu 'alayhi wa sallam, told us in one of the narrations that the (righteous) slave calls upon his Lord in the grave, saying: *"O Allaah, bring the Hour"*.[1] so that he can see his family and wealth. This is because a window towards Paradise would be opened for him while he is in his grave and he will be able to see its bliss and joy. He will be told: *"Sleep like the sleep of a bride, whom no one would wake up except the dearest of his family members to him."* [2]

As for the disbelievers, they will be terrified in their graves and wish that the Hour will never come. This is because of the terrible torment that they will face in their graves, and because they will know the severity of the punishment which is awaiting them.

Allaah The Almighty Said about Fir'awn (Pharaoh), his people and his soldiers (what means): *{The Fire: they are exposed to it morning and evening.[3] And the Day the Hour appears [it*

---

1 Reported by Ahmad (18557) and Al-Albaani classed it as authentic.
2 Reported by At-Tirmithi (1071) and Al-Albaani classed it as authentic.
3 From the time of their death until the Day of Resurrection, when they will be driven into it.

will be said]. 'Make the people of Pharaoh enter the severest punishment.'} [QUR'AAN 12:87] **They are now in their graves and their fear is increasing because they are exposed to the fire everyday and know very well their final abode and their destiny; how great would their fear then be?**

- **When would placing one's hope in people become Shirk (associating partners with Allaah)?**

The highest level of hope is when one places his hope in Allaah The Almighty and none in humans. One may have some hope in humans, like having hope that a certain man may be able to help one due to his lofty rank within a community, or due to his wealth or position. This is something which one can hardly escape. However, the important question is: when does placing hope in humans become major Shirk?

Ibn Taymiyyah, may Allaah have mercy upon him, said: "Anyone who equals Allaah to His slaves in love, hope or fear has committed Shirk." [1]

Therefore, this is the rule: if one makes his hope in humans equal to that in Allaah The Almighty, then he has committed major Shirk. Thus one should be careful and struggle against oneself to stay away from this feeling, so that Allaah The Almighty may protect us from punishment.

---

1 Majmoo' Al-Fataawa (339/27).

Conclusion

A believer must combine hope and fear in his servitude to Allaah The Almighty, in order to achieve his sought objectives and have his needs fulfilled.

Al-Manaawi, may Allaah have mercy upon him, said: "Fear and hope are two arrows of servitude; fear represents a need, while hope represents weakness. Servitude to Allaah will become pure either by fear of one's shortcomings, or gratitude for being able to perform good deeds. Remembering [one's] shortcomings necessitates fear and seeing that he is enabled to perform good deeds necessitates hope." [1]

A Muslim should stay away from feeling despair of the mercy of Allaah The Almighty and must always think good of his Lord. Al-Manaawi, may Allaah have mercy upon him, said: "Despairing of the mercy of Allaah lessens one's chances of receiving the mercy and the blessings of Allaah, and this is why it is considered one of the acts that are pronounced as major Shirk committed by the heart. Having hope in Allaah and thinking good of Him are among the greatest provisions that one can have in his journey towards Allaah." [2]

---

1 Faydh Al-Qadeer (315/3).
2 Faydh Al-Qadeer (455/6).

The one who assesses himself should not blind himself from seeing his mistakes and shortcomings and continue committing them, claiming to have hope in Allaah The Almighty and His mercy. Abu Al-Wafaa' ibn 'Aqeel, may Allaah have mercy upon him, said: "Beware and do not be deceived; a hand is cut off for stealing three Dirhams' worth, the penalty of lashes is applied if one drinks as little as the head of a needle of intoxicants, a woman was thrown into Hell for (torturing) a cat and a martyr was burnt in his grave for stealing a small garment." [1]

Do not be a person who does not have hope, because you will then be as one who is dead. Ibn Al-'Alaa`, may Allaah have mercy upon him, said: "Brother in Islaam, you should know that the deeds of the heart are connected to each other, and so whenever any of these deeds becomes stronger, the other deeds of the heart get influenced by it, and whenever any of these deeds becomes weaker, the other deeds of the heart also get influenced by it."

Ibn Taymiyyah, may Allaah have mercy upon him, said: "Know that there are three deeds (of the heart) that bring the person closer to Allaah: fear, hope and love, and the strongest of all these is love. Fear is intended to prevent one from deviating from the path. Love is what motivates and pushes the person on to move towards the One he loves, and the stronger the love is the more steadfast his steps towards his Beloved become. Fear prevents the person from deviating from the path that delivers

---

1 Al-Jawaab Al-Kaafi (21).

him to his Beloved, while hope leads him to the One he loves. This is a great principle which the slave should be heedful of, because his servitude to Allaah will not be established without fulfilling it, and everyone should be a slave of Allaah alone and no one else." [1]

Brother in Islaam, you should know that paying attention to one of the deeds of the heart while neglecting other deeds leads a person to misguidance and error. Ibn Taymiyyah, may Allaah have mercy upon him, said: "Some pious people said, 'He who worships Allaah with love only is a Murji' [as mentioned previously, a deviant sect which believes that faith is in the heart and acting upon it is not part of faith, and that faith never increases or decreases and that man creates his own deeds]. He who worships Allaah with fear only is a Haroori [a group of the deviant sect of Khawaarij which claims that one becomes a disbeliever and will eternally dwell in Hell if he commits a major sin and they also claim that the Qur'aan is created and is not one of the attributes of Allaah. They also reject any Prophetic text that contradicts reason]. And he who worships Allaah with love only is a Zindeeq [e.g. the Sufis]. But he who worships Allaah with fear, love and hope is a true Muwahhid [a believer who is upon Tawheed (Islamic monotheism)]." [2]

O Allaah, protect us and have mercy upon us and accept our

---

1 Majmoo' Al-Fataawa (95/1).
2 Majmoo' Al-Fataawa (81/10).

supplications as we have no hope in anyone other than You; You are sufficient for us and The Best to rely upon.

Test yourself

The following are some questions on the subject of hope. The questions are divided into two levels; one is straightforward, and the other requires a deep look and reflection before answering.

The first level:

- What is the difference between hope and wishful thinking?
- Mention four fruits of having hope in Allaah The Almighty.
- Mention things that help establish hope.
- Mention a verse from the Qur'aan that combines between fear and hope.
- When should a believer make fear dominate hope?
- When should a believer make hope dominate fear?
- List the types of praised and dispraised hope.
- What are the levels of hope?
- What are the signs indicating the soundness of one's hope?
- What are the feelings that move and motivate the heart?

The second level:

- What is the meaning of the following statement: "Everyone who has hope has fear, and everyone who has fear has hope"?
- Mention things that help establish hope other than what was mentioned in this book?
- Is hope a cure? If yes, explain how.
- Mention the principle which one must fulfill in his heart regarding hope and fear?
- Why is the frequent mention of Allaah considered to be one of the fruits of hope?
- What is despair, and how can a Muslim stay away from it?
- When would having hope in humans part of major *Shirk*?
- Is hope limited to matters related to the Hereafter? Explain how.
- How can one avoid wishful thinking?